MATHS
Practice for
Key Stage 2
National tests
ges 9-10

TEST
YOUR CHIl
MATHS

Parent's Booklet

**Test A and Mental Arithmetic
Test Booklet pull-out**

Test B and Test C Booklet pull-out

Let's learn at home
MATHS

INTRODUCTION

What are the Key Stage 2 National Tests?

Every year in May, children in Year 6 (the final year of primary school or midway through middle school) take written National Tests. There are two English, three maths and two science tests. They are designed to show the levels of work your child is able to achieve in these three core subjects. The tests are carried out over one week. The papers are marked by external examiners. When returned to school, the results of the tests (commonly known as SATs) give parents and teachers an indication of each child's knowledge in relation to the standards set out in the National Curriculum (NC). They also provide a rough guide to how your child's school has performed in relation to other schools both locally and nationally.

What the test results mean

Along with assessments made by the class teacher, your child's National Test results will be sent to his or her secondary school and be used by the staff there to help them decide the most appropriate teaching groups for your child to be placed in.

About the maths tests

During the test week, your child will take three separate maths tests at school. The first two (Tests A and B) will each last 45 minutes and be taken on different days. The third is a mental arithmetic test with about 20 quick-fire questions with varying times allowed for answering. These tests cover NC Levels 3–5 and the questions increase in difficulty through the paper. Under exceptional circumstances, and at the discretion of the teacher, a very able child can be entered for an additional Level 6 extension test lasting 30 minutes (Test C).

The mathematics National Curriculum is divided up into: (Ma1) Using and Applying Mathematics; (Ma2) Number; (Ma3) Shape, Space and Measures; (Ma4) Handling Data. Each section has a Programme of Study setting out what should be taught and Attainment Targets for expected standards or levels of performance. This is mirrored in the test structure.

The National Tests exclude the testing of 'Using and Applying Mathematics' and concentrate on testing your child's knowledge and understanding of number, shape and data handling. 'Using and Applying Mathematics' will be assessed by your child's class teacher, but is still very important. The sections do not have equal proportions of the test marks. In Tests A and B, 'Number' has the most questions and accounts for nearly half of the total number of marks available on the test papers. 'Shape, Space and Measures' and 'Handling Data' share about an equal proportion of the remaining questions and marks. The mental arithmetic marks account for about 20 per cent (one fifth) of the total marks available in the tests.

How this book can help you to help your child

The practice papers in this book can help you prepare your child in the most realistic way possible for the end of Key Stage 2 National Tests in maths. They will help to:

- familiarize your child with the format and layout of test papers
- familiarize your child with the type of questions in the tests
- indicate areas of strength or weakness
- approximate for you the level your child is working at in maths.

The 'Tips to Help Your Child' notes which accompany the answers to Tests A and B provide suggestions for ways in which you can help to improve your child's progress and performance, not only with the questions on the test papers, but also in associated mathematical areas.

Using this book

This book is made up from three booklets, each one separately stapled. Pull out the centre booklet first. This contains Tests B and C. Next pull out the booklet containing Test A and the child's answer sheet for the Mental Arithmetic Test. The remaining booklet has background information, test answers/helpful tips, the Mental Arithmetic Test and conversion information for changing your child's test scores into National Curriculum Levels.

Parent's Booklet

Taking the tests

Before you set the test
It is important that your child feels comfortable about sitting these practice papers. Explain that they should help him or her to become used to the kinds of activities in the actual tests.

At the start
Your child should take Test A first, then Test B and finally the Mental Arithmetic Test. Test C should only be attempted if your child scores a combined mark of 100 or more on the three main tests. Do each test on a separate day, at a time when your child is not tired or irritable, and in a quiet place with no distractions. Make sure you allow plenty of time for taking, marking and talking afterwards about the test. Be as positive as you can so that your child starts each test confidently. It is important he or she should not feel over-anxious or pressured. If your child shows any signs of distress, leave the test until a later date. Finally, read the instructions together carefully and ensure your child understands them.

During the test
How rigidly you observe the time-limits for these practice tests depends on how far you wish to replicate the actual test conditions. You may wish to insist on your child working entirely alone, asking no questions. Or you may prefer not to put your child under the pressure of keeping strictly to 'test conditions'. Working through practice papers is a perfectly valid test preparation activity. You could help your child increase speed by giving extra practice later. As with any skill, the more practice you have, the more efficient you become.

For Tests A, B and C, make sure he or she has a pencil, ruler and a clock or watch for timing the test. For Tests B and C, your child will also need a protractor and may use a calculator. For the Mental Arithmetic Test, the instructions can be found on page 12 of this booklet.

Once your child has started, don't fuss and keep looking over his or her shoulder. If your child finishes before the end of the test time, encourage him or her to go back and check answers. If your child does not finish before the time is up, stop the test, make a note of where your child is up to, then allow your child to finish the test, if he or she wishes. However, only that part of the test finished during the allowed time should be marked for the final test score.

Marking the answers

Mark all the tests with your child present. If your child gets an answer wrong, go over the question and try to discover how the mistake was made. If he or she did not attempt the question at all, discuss the problem and see if you can elicit a correct answer by phrasing the question differently. The important thing is to try to encourage children to 'think' for themselves. Don't just tell your child the answers. This is of no benefit at all.

Marking Tests A, B and C
Use the mark schemes provided on pages 5–11 to award marks as indicated. The arrangement of the answers is fairly clear, but you may have to use your discretion occasionally!

● In the margin of each test paper, there is a mark box alongside each question part. Write the number of marks scored by your child for that part of the question in this box. If your child gets the question wrong, put '0' in the box. If your child does not attempt the question, put a '–' in the box. Do not leave any mark box empty.

● At the bottom of all the right-hand page margins is a 'total' box for the number of marks scored on that double (or single) page. Write each of these totals on to the 'marking grid' on the front cover of the test booklet and add them up.

● Transfer the final total mark to the correct text column of the first table on the inside back cover of this booklet.

Marking the Mental Arithmetic Test

The mark scheme for the Mental Arithmetic Test is on page 11 of this booklet. In the mark boxes, write either '1' for a correct response or '0' for an incorrect response. Total up the marks and write the score in the space provided on your child's answer sheet. Then transfer this mark to the correct test column on the first table on the inside back cover of this booklet.

Using the 'Tips to help your child'

Each answer page for Tests A and B includes suggestions for ways in which you can help to improve your child's test performance if you find that he or she is having particular difficulty with either a specific area of the maths curriculum or a specific question type. You may, of course, have some ideas of your own on how to help your child. If you do, always beware of causing confusion if any 'help' is different from what your child has been taught in school.

What do National Curriculum Levels mean?

For children between the ages of 5 and 14 the National Curriculum is divided into eight levels of attainment. Children are expected to advance approximately one level for every two years they are at school. At the end of Key Stage 1, children are expected to be working at Level 2. By the end of Key Stage 2, it is expected they will be at Level 4. The table shows you at what level an average child should be working for each of the six years of primary school.

Key Stage	Year	NC Level
1	1	1
1	2	2
2	3	2/3
2	4	3
2	5	3/4
2	6	4/5

The questions in Tests A and B and the Mental Arithmetic Test in this book cater for children working at NC Levels 2–4. Extension Test C caters for children working at NC Level 5, but should only be taken by your child if he or she scores a combined mark of 100 or more in the three main tests. After you have marked the test papers in this book, follow the instructions on the inside back cover to work out your child's National Curriculum Level.

Important note

In marking National Test papers, external markers use their professional judgement, based on years of experience. It is not to be expected that as a parent you will be able to bring the same experience and judgement to marking these practice papers. The marks you award and the level your child gains as a result of doing these practice papers may therefore differ from those that examiners or teachers at your child's school would give. Please remember too that the purpose of this book is to provide test practice for your child, as well as to highlight any areas of difficulty he or she may be having. We suggest that you use the information about your child's performance in these practice papers as a basis for discussion with your child's teacher, who will be able to offer advice and ideas for helping your child to improve in areas of need.

Answers to Test A

Q		MARKS

1. Award 1 mark each for a and b only if both calculations are correct. **2**

a. 15, 18

b. 19, 16

2. Award 1 mark for any three shapes correctly identified to a maximum of 2 marks. **2**

pentagon

circle

hexagon

triangle

rectangle

square

3.

a. Award 1 mark if all eight numbers are in order **1** starting with the smallest (credit the mark if the cm units are missing but not if the numbers start with the largest).

13cm, 25cm, 36cm, 48cm, 52cm, 71cm, 84cm, 97cm

Award 1 mark each for b and c correctly answered (credit each mark if the cm units are missing). **2**

b. 84cm

c. 74cm

4. Award 1 mark each for a–c (credit answers with spelling mistakes but not answers with the p sign missing). **3**

a. lolly

b. 30p

c. 10p

5. Award 1 mark for each correct set of missing numbers.

a. 9, 21, 24 **1**

b. 18, 12, 8 **1**

6.

a. Award 1 mark for the five lines correctly measured (credit the mark if the cm units are missing). **1**

5cm, 8cm, 12cm, 10cm, 7cm

b. Award 1 mark for the five lengths of line correctly drawn. Ruler drawn lines of the following lengths should be shown. **1**

3cm, 6cm, 11cm, 9cm, 4cm

7.

a. Award 1 mark if all the required numbers are circled. **1**

These numbers should be circled.

8, 26, 20, 46, 28, 50, 14, 16, 32, 4, 30, 24

b. Award 1 mark if all the squares and circles are connected correctly. **1** *(continued page 6)*

Tips to help your child – Test A

Encourage your child to look for number 'bonds' or pairs that make '10'. Regular oral daily practice adding single-digit numbers is a useful method of improving addition speed and accuracy. On a car journey, invent a game that requires your child to add the digits found on car registration plates.

Your child should be familiar with the names and properties of all the plane or 2-D shapes illustrated in the question. He or she should be able to identify each of these shapes from a written or oral description of their key features. Looking for and identifying different shapes in everyday surroundings is a positive way of helping to reinforce the names and characteristics of the more common shapes – for example, looking at cereal boxes, company logos, the shapes on the outside of a house, and so on.

Practise ordering other groups of numbers less than 100. You could use a till receipt and ask your child to write the amounts less than £1 in order, starting with the most/least expensive item.

One way of helping to improve your child's understanding of data displayed as a graph is to ask your child to keep a personal record of how he/she spends his/her own pocket money and to record the information in a similar way to the block graph illustrated. Also, look out for information displayed as graphs in shops, magazines and so on, and discuss with your child what the information means.

These patterns are made by (a) adding 3, and (b) subtracting 2. Similar missing number exercises will help your child. Use numbers in the 2, 3, 4, 5 and 10 times tables in both ascending and descending steps.

Draw lines of varying lengths up to 30cm for your child to measure. Make sure that all the lines are in whole centimetre lengths to begin with but later on introduce lengths to the nearest half centimetre. Develop this activity into the child drawing lines of specified length. Insist on accuracy and the use of a ruler. You could also give your child a list of common objects around the house and ask him or her to measure them to the nearest centimetre.

Point out to your child that answers to the 2, 4 and 10 times tables are always even numbers, while the answers to the 3 and 5 times tables have both odd and even answers. Practise the 2, 3, 4, 5 and 10 times tables regularly with your child beyond the tenth multiple. Try to reach the stage with your child whereby if you say any number less than 100 he or she *(continued page 6)*

| Q | Answers | MARKS | Tips |

will be able to tell you which of the above tables it occurs in.

Using oral methods, test regularly to make sure that your child knows all the doubles of numbers up to 10 + 10 and then in stages over a period of time help him or her to build up his or her knowledge of doubles for all numbers up to 20 + 20.

8. Award 1 mark each for a–d. **4**
a. 20, 15, 35
b. 60
c. thirty
d. five

Check that your child has not overlooked the key that accompanies the pictogram. Doing so will result in the answers to all sections of the question being incorrect. Ask your child to make up his or her own pictogram on which to record information of his or her own choice, where one symbol represents several items or people.

9. Award 1 mark for both a and b if all the pairs of numbers are connected correctly. **2**
a. (26p–34p) (35p–43p) (41p–49p)
b. (£12–£6) (£33–£27) (£29–£23) (£45–£39)

Orally practise adding/subtracting any single-digit number to/from any double-digit number up to 50. Start by not crossing the tens column so there is no 'borrowing' involved. Cross the tens column at a later stage to include 'borrowing'.

10. Award 1 mark if both shapes are successfully drawn. **1**
Accept any two different shapes that have nine squares shaded.

Squared paper will enable your child to carry out similar activities to those found in this question. Areas up to about 20cm² can be attempted.

11. Award 1 mark for any two correct answers a–h up to a maximum of 4 marks (credit answers with the units of measure missing). **4**
a. 18p
b. £20
c. 24g
d. 5
e. 46g
f. 25p
g. £52
h. 78

Questions with missing numbers are very popular in test papers. Make up sets of your own questions to give to your child. At a very simple level (single-digit numbers) the questions can be asked orally, but as the difficulty increases the child needs to have the questions written in front of him or her so that reference can be made to the numbers involved as required. At this level of work keep to numbers under 100 and have the missing number in all three positions (see question 11). Try and emphasize the fact that if you know two numbers in a calculation you can always find the third by carrying out one of the remaining four rules of number with the two numbers that you know. Point out that +/– and ×/÷ are 'inverse' or 'opposite' operations and can 'undo' each other.

12. Award 1 mark for a correctly completed chart. **1**

Child's name	Starting time	Finishing time
Laura	10.45am	11.15am
David	1.15pm	1.45pm
Lisa	3.00pm	3.30pm
Sean	11.30am	12.00am

Opportunities arise frequently for your child to tell the time. Calculations involving time frequently cause children problems, especially when spanning the full hour. Practice with time difference questions should concentrate first on full hours and then lead on gradually to questions involving half hours, minutes in multiples of five and finally measurement in minutes that cross the hour barrier. Knowledge of both the 12 and 24 hour clock systems is required at this level as is familiarity with both the traditional clock-face and the digital readout.

13. Award 1 mark each for a–c. **3**
a. 280
b. 50
c. 31

Make up function machine questions of your own. Try and use all four 'operations' (+, –, ×, ÷) and start with easy questions.

14. Award 1 mark each for a–c. **3**
a. 26
b. Class 3
c. 30

Go over the chart with your child. Ask him or her some additional questions related to the information given. If you have time, accompany your child to do a survey of his or her own. For instance, you could visit three different streets and ask your child to record how many cars of certain colours are parked there.

MATHS
Practice for
Key Stage 2
National tests
ages 9-10

MARKING GRID

Page	Marks possible	Marks scored
2–3	7	
4–5	7	
6–7	6	
8–9	8	
10–11	9	
12–13	6	
14–15	7	
TOTAL	50	

Let's learn at home
MATHS

Test A Booklet

CALCULATOR NOT ALLOWED

For this test you will need a **pencil**, a **ruler** and a **watch** or **clock** to time yourself. Sit at a table in a quiet place.

Ask an adult to read through the test instructions with you before you start.

INSTRUCTIONS

1. You will have **45 minutes** to do this test.
2. Work as quickly and as carefully as possible.
3. Do not worry if you cannot finish all the questions. Do as many as you can.
4. If you wish to change an answer, cross it out and write your new answer next to it.
5. Do not waste time on a question you cannot do. Move on to the next one.
6. Read the instructions carefully and write your answers in the spaces highlighted by the pencil symbol.
7. Some pages have 'working out areas'. Use these spaces for doing your working out. If you need to do further working out, use any other empty space on the page.
8. Move straight on from one page to the next without waiting to be told.
9. Once you have started the test you must not talk to anyone or ask any questions.
10. If there is time left when you have finished, check your answers and try to do any questions you missed out earlier.

First Name

Last Name

1. Add up each set of three numbers.

a.

5	4	6

3	8	7

1a

1 mark

b.

5	9	5

6	2	8

1b

1 mark

2. Using a pencil line, join each 2-D shape to the correct name label.

pentagon   square   hexagon

2

2 marks

circle   rectangle   triangle

3. David has eight pieces of string. Here are their lengths.

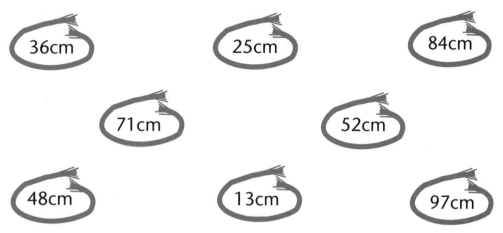

36cm   25cm   84cm

71cm   52cm

48cm   13cm   97cm

a. Put David's pieces of string in order, starting with the shortest length.

Shortest

Longest

3a

1 mark

b. Take away the shortest length of string from the longest.

cm

WORKING OUT AREA

3b

1 mark

c. Add together the three shortest lengths of string.

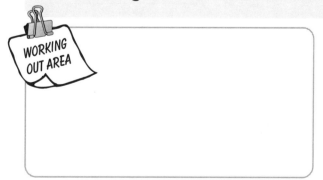

WORKING OUT AREA

cm

3c

1 mark

TOTAL

3

4. This graph shows how Tessa spends her pocket money.

a. Which item cost twice as much as the eraser?

4a

1 mark

_____

b. Write down the cost of the comic.

4b

1 mark

_____

c. How much more did the crisps cost than the pencil?

4c

1 mark

_____

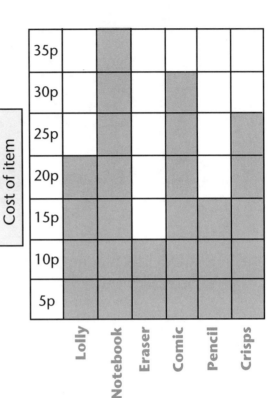

Cost of item

| 35p |
| 30p |
| 25p |
| 20p |
| 15p |
| 10p |
| 5p |

Lolly | Notebook | Eraser | Comic | Pencil | Crisps

Name of item

WORKING OUT AREA

5. Fill in the missing numbers in these patterns.

5a

1 mark

a. 3   6   ☐   12   15   18   ☐   ☐   27

5b

1 mark

b. 20   ☐   16   14   ☐   10   ☐   6

6a. Measure the length of each line. Give each answer in **cm**.

6a
1 mark

b. Next to each box, draw a line the length that is indicated.

3cm

6cm

11cm

9cm

4cm

6b
1 mark

TOTAL

7a. Circle all the numbers that are answers to the 2 times table.

7a

1 mark

| 8 | 26 | 35 | 41 | 20 | 15 |

| 46 | 33 | 19 | 7 | 39 | 28 |

| 50 | 25 | 23 | 14 | 16 | 32 |

| 4 | 30 | 37 | 43 | 24 | 21 |

b. Join each number in a square to its double in a circle.

7b

1 mark

2   10   8   6

    5   9   6

16   4

    18   8   4

        14   3   12

7

6

8. This chart shows how many packets of cakes were sold by a shop on each day one week.

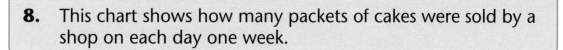

➝ 5 packets	
Number of packets of cakes sold	
Monday	🧁 🧁
Tuesday	🧁 🧁 🧁
Wednesday	🧁 🧁 🧁 🧁 🧁 🧁 🧁 🧁 🧁 🧁
Thursday	🧁 🧁 🧁 🧁 🧁 🧁 🧁 🧁
Friday	🧁 🧁 🧁 🧁
Saturday	🧁 🧁 🧁 🧁 🧁 🧁 🧁
Sunday	🧁 🧁 🧁 🧁 🧁

How many packets of cakes were sold on:

a. Friday? ⬚   Tuesday? ⬚   Saturday? ⬚

b. Monday and Wednesday combined? ⬚

Write down the answers to these questions in words.

c. How many more packets were sold on Wednesday than on Friday? _____

d. How many fewer packets were sold on Monday than on Tuesday? _____

WORKING OUT AREA

8a

1 mark

8b

1 mark

8c

1 mark

8d

1 mark

TOTAL

Let's learn at home
MATHS

Test A
Booklet

9a

1 mark

9b

1 mark

10

1 mark

9. Connect each amount on the left to an amount on the right in the way that is indicated.

a.   is 8p less than      **b.**   is £6 more than

8p	49p	£12	£23
26p	16p	£33	£27
35p	43p	£29	£39
41p	34p	£45	£6

WORKING OUT AREA

10. On grid A shade in an area of **9cm²**.

On grid B shade in a different shape that has the same area.

A.

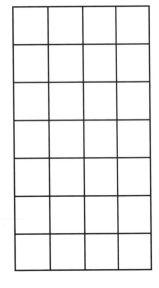

B.

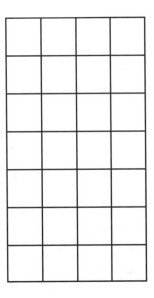

MATHS
Practice for Key Stage 2 National tests
ages 9-10

MARKING GRID

Page	Marks possible	Marks scored
2–3	8	
4–5	5	
6–7	7	
8–9	9	
10–11	9	
12–13	6	
14	6	
TOTAL	50	

Test B Booklet

CALCULATOR ALLOWED

For this test you will need a **pencil**, a **ruler**, a **protractor** and a **watch** or **clock** to time yourself. You may also have a **calculator** if you wish. Sit at a table in a quiet place.

Ask an adult to read through the test instructions with you before you start.

INSTRUCTIONS

1. You will have **45 minutes** to do this test.
2. Work as quickly and as carefully as possible.
3. Do not worry if you do not finish all the questions. Do as many as you can.
4. If you wish to change an answer, cross it out and write your new answer next to it.
5. Do not waste time on a question you cannot do. Move on to the next one.
6. Read the instructions carefully and write your answers in the spaces highlighted by the pencil symbol.
7. If you need to do any working out, use a 'working out area' or any other empty space on the page.
8. Move straight on from one page to the next without waiting to be told.
9. Once you have started the test, you must not talk to anyone or ask any questions.
10. If there is time left when you have finished, check your answers and try to do any questions you missed out earlier.

First Name

Last Name

MATHS

Test B
Booklet

1a

1 mark

1b

1 mark

1. Fill in the answers to these problems.

a. 12 + 5 = ☐

b. 6 + 13 = ☐

8 ÷ 2 = ☐

58 – 7 = ☐

9 – 6 = ☐

3 × 5 = ☐

WORKING OUT AREA

2a

1 mark

2a. Work out the total cost of both items.   ☐

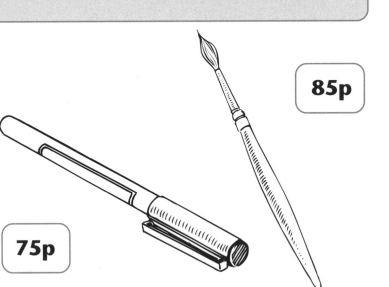

85p

75p

2b

1 mark

b. If you bought both items, how much change would you have from £2.00?   ☐

3a. Look at the shapes below.
Put a cross on one right angle in each shape.

Test B
Booklet

3a

1 mark

b. Study the grid below.

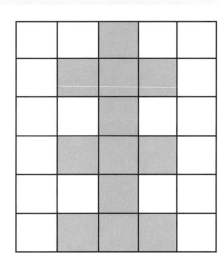

How many shaded squares are there on the grid?

_____

How many more white squares are there than black squares on the grid?

_____

3b

2 marks

c. Follow the instructions to find a way through the maze.
Show the way you go with a pencil line.

Go forward 3 squares and turn left.
Go forward 1 square and turn right.
Go forward 2 squares and turn left.
Go forward 1 square and turn right.
Go forward 1 square.

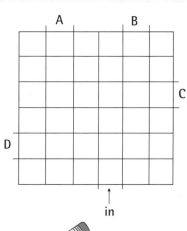

A   B

C

D

↑
in

3c

1 mark

At which letter do you leave the maze? _____

TOTAL

3

4. The data in this box gives the colours of the cars in a car park.

Car colour	Number of cars
Red (R)	5
Blue (B)	2
Green (G)	6
Yellow (Y)	1
Brown (Bn)	4
Grey (Gy)	3

a. Use the data to fill in the block graph below.

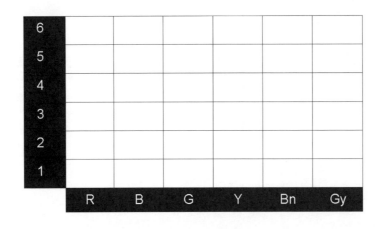

Car colour

b. How many more red cars are there than yellow cars?

_____

c. How many fewer brown cars are there than green cars?

_____

4a

1 mark

4b

1 mark

4c

1 mark

4

5. Join these numbers in order. Start from the largest.

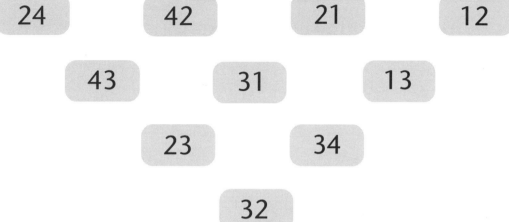

24   42   21   12

43   31   13

23   34

32

6. Look at this calendar month carefully and then answer the questions below.

		August			
Mon		6	13	20	27
Tues		7	14	21	28
Wed	1	8	15	22	29
Thurs	2	9	16	23	30
Fri	3	10	17	24	31
Sat	4	11	18	25	
Sun	5	12	19	26	

How many days are there in August? _____

On this calendar, what day is the 19th of August? _____

What are the dates on this calendar of all the Fridays in August?

_____

7. Look at this Venn diagram and then answer the questions about it below.

odd numbers

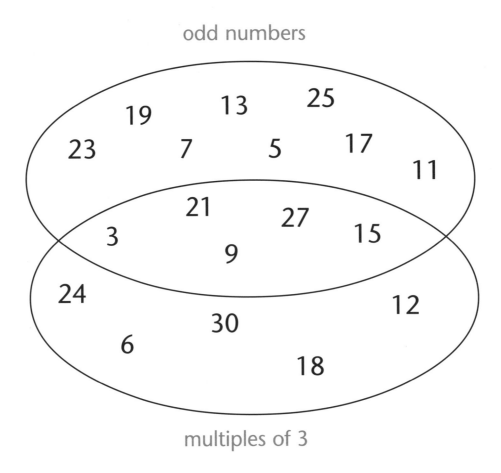

multiples of 3

a. Which numbers are both **odd** numbers and multiples of 3?

7a

1 mark

_____

b. Which numbers are **even** numbers and multiples of 3?

7b

1 mark

_____

c. Write down any multiples of 2 that are shown on the Venn diagram.

7c

1 mark

_____

6

8. Listed below are the entrance prices to the **World of Fear Fun Park**.

World of Fear Fun Park	Open daily from 09.00 to 18.00	
	Weekdays	Weekends
Adult	£8.00	£9.50
Senior citizen	£5.50	£7.00
Child (5 – 16yrs)	£4.50	£6.00
Under 5s	Free	Free

Use the price list to work out the cost of these visits to the Park.

a. Two adults on a Sunday.

b. Three senior citizens on a Friday.

c. An adult and two children aged 9 and 11 on a Saturday.

d. One adult and three children aged 3, 5 and 12 on a weekday.

WORKING OUT AREA

Let's learn at home
MATHS
Test B
Booklet

9a. Some of the shapes named below have curved faces
and some have flat faces. Some have both!
Group each shape into the correct column on the chart.

cuboid

cylinder

cube

cone

pyramid

sphere

flat faces only	curved faces only	flat and curved faces

9a

1 mark

9b

b. Name any item you can think of
that is the same shape as a sphere.

_____

1 mark

10. Mum uses a third of these mug mats on the kitchen table.

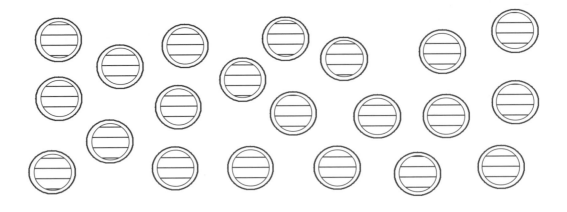

10a

a. How many mats does she use?

1 mark

10b

b. How many mats are left over?

1 mark

11. The pictogram shows the number of rounders scored by three players in a season. Use this information to answer the questions.

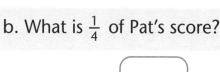

means 150 rounders

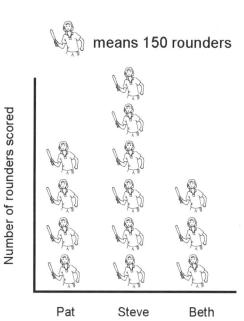

Number of rounders scored

Pat   Steve   Beth

a. What is $\frac{1}{2}$ of Steve's score?

11a

1 mark

b. What is $\frac{1}{4}$ of Pat's score?

11b

1 mark

c. What is $\frac{1}{3}$ of Beth's score?

11c

1 mark

WORKING OUT AREA

12. Join up each sum on the left to the correct answer on the right.
The first one has been done for you.

a.

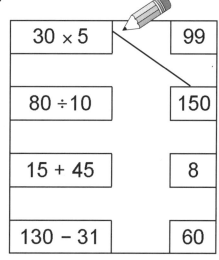

30 × 5		99
80 ÷ 10		150
15 + 45		8
130 − 31		60

b.

57 − 27		35
23 + 12		22
24 ÷ 3		8
2 × 11		30

12a

1 mark

12b

1 mark

TOTAL

MATHS

Test B
Booklet

13. Look at these numbers and then answer the questions about them.

374   347   734

473   743

a. What is 347 to the nearest 10? Write your answer in words.

13a

1 mark

13b

b. What is 743 to the nearest 100?

1 mark

13c

c. One more number can be made using the digits 3, 7 and 4. What is that number?

1 mark

14a. Mark these points on the grid with an **X**.

(2, 1) (5, 1) (5, 4) (2, 4)

14a

1 mark

Join up the points in this order.
(2, 1) to (5, 1), (5, 1) to (5, 4)
(5, 4) to (2, 4), (2, 4) to (2, 1)

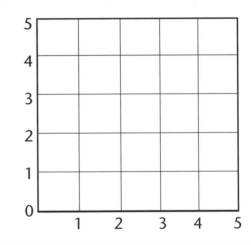

14b

b. Name the shape you have just drawn.

1 mark

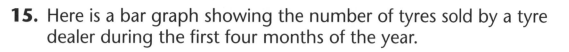

15. Here is a bar graph showing the number of tyres sold by a tyre dealer during the first four months of the year.

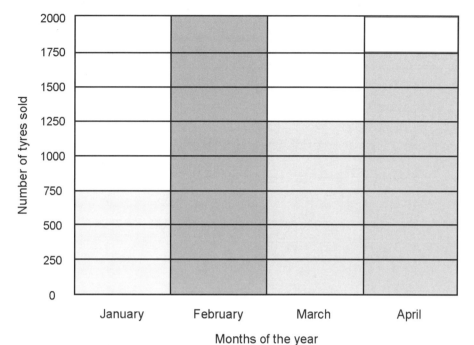

a. How many more tyres were sold in April than in March?

WORKING OUT AREA

_____

b. Work out the total number of tyres sold during all four months.

_____

15a

1 mark

15b

1 mark

16a. Three lengths are cut from a 14 metre length of carpet.
The lengths are 3.90m, 5.05m and 2.75m.
What length of carpet is left over?

_____

b. Sketch books are 4mm thick. They are packed in bundles of 144.
Work out the total thickness of 5 bundles.

_____

16a

1 mark

16b

1 mark

TOTAL

17. On the grid, draw and shade in a shape that has a perimeter of 32 centimetres (cm).

17

1 mark

18. Fifteen children in Year 5 at North Road School held a competition to see who could put the most daisies into a chain in 5 minutes.
Here are their results.

Number of daisies into a chain in 5 minutes				
13	24	26	21	16
32	28	25	13	24
14	24	28	28	8

Study the data above and then use it to complete the table.

Number of daisies	Tally	Frequency
0–8		
9–16		4
17–24	| |||	
25–32		

18

2 marks

19. John has been looking at the prices of some sporting equipment.

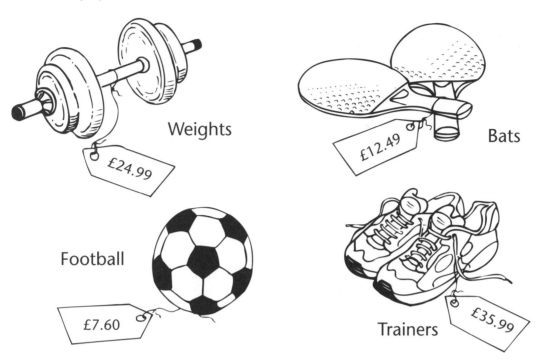

Weights £24.99

Bats £12.49

Football £7.60

Trainers £35.99

a. John spent £56.08 on three items of equipment.
Which three items did he buy?

19a

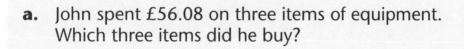

1 mark

b. John pays for the items with
three £20 notes.
How much change does he receive?

19b

1 mark

c. What is the difference in price between
the weights and the trainers?

19c

1 mark

 WORKING OUT AREA

TOTAL

Test B
Booklet

20a. How many 63-seater coaches will be needed to carry 384 children?

20a

1 mark

It costs each child £1.25 to travel on the coach.

20b

1 mark

b. Work out the total travelling cost for all the children.

WORKING OUT AREA

21. Fill in the missing numbers in these problems.

21a

1 mark

21b

1 mark

a. 46 + ☐ = 58 + 62   **b.** ☐ × 24 = 12 × 12

22a

1 mark

22. Complete these number sequences.

22b

1 mark

a.   3   5   8   12   ☐

TOTAL

b.   25   19   14   10   ☐

STOP HERE

14

MARKING GRID

Page	Marks possible	Marks scored
1	5	
2–3	12	
4–5	14	
6	9	
TOTAL	40	

Test C

CALCULATOR ALLOWED

For this test you will need a **pencil**, a **ruler**, a **protractor** and a **watch** or **clock**.
You may also have a **calculator** if you wish.

The instructions for this test are the same as for **Test B** except that you are only allowed **30 minutes** to answer the questions.
Go over **Test B** instructions 2–10 again with an adult.

---

1. Find the following amounts.

a. 30% of 590 [ ]

c. $\frac{7}{10}$ of 5700 [ ]

b. 70% of 330 [ ]

d. $\frac{3}{8}$ of 8040 [ ]

1

4 marks

---

2. When two different numbers are added together they equal 30.
When they are multiplied together they equal 221.

What are the two numbers? [ ]

2

1 mark

WORKING OUT AREA

TOTAL

1

Let's learn at home
MATHS

Test C
Booklet

3a

2 marks

3b

2 marks

3c

2 marks

4a

1 mark

4b

1 mark

3a. Round these numbers to the nearest 100.

WORKING OUT AREA

1960cm _____   56 550m _____

b. Round these numbers to the nearest 1000.

6380g _____   £49 728 _____

c. Do these calculations using pencil and paper methods.

```
    1 3 5
  ×   2 9
  _____
```

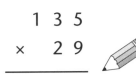

```
      _____
4 5 | 6 7 5
```

WORKING OUT AREA

4. These are the number of points scored by two school teams in one term.

Red team 380 points

Blue team 420 points

Three fifths of red team points were scored by girls.

a. How many points did the girls in the red team score?

60% of blue team points were scored by boys.

b. How many points did the boys in the blue team score?

5. Work out the area and the perimeter of these 2-D shapes.

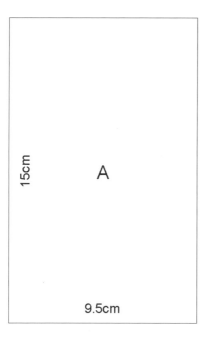

15cm

A

9.5cm

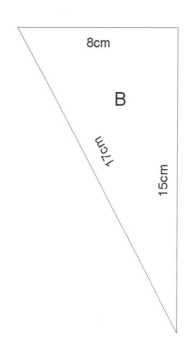

8cm

B

17cm

15cm

a. Area of Shape A equals [ ] cm²

5a

1 mark

b. Area of Shape B equals [ ] cm²

5b

1 mark

c. Perimeter of Shape A equals [ ] cm

5c

1 mark

d. Perimeter of Shape B equals [ ] cm

5d

1 mark

WORKING OUT AREA

TOTAL

3

6. This table shows the temperature at daybreak on the same day in five different European cities.

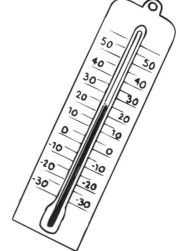

City	Temp ^{0}C
Copenhagen	-3^0
Stockholm	-9^0
Oslo	-14^0
Brussels	$+8^0$
Rome	$+17^0$

6a

1 mark

a. What is the difference in temperature between Rome and Stockholm?

6b

1 mark

b. By how many °C would the temperature in Copenhagen have to drop to be equivalent to the temperature in Oslo?

Five hours later the temperature in Oslo has risen by 8°C and the temperature in Brussels has risen by 11°C.

6c

1 mark

c. What is the difference in temperature now between the two cities?

7a

1 mark

7a. Measure this angle and write your answer in the box.

o

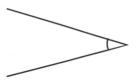

7b

1 mark

b. Is the angle an ACUTE, OBTUSE or REFLEX angle?

8. In each of the four boxes below, write a different number so that the **mean** of the four numbers is 7.

9. There are 216 yachts in a marina.
The **pie chart** shows their colours.

a. What percentage of the yachts are blue?

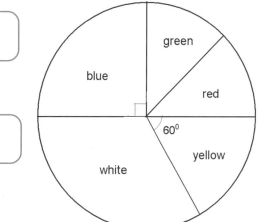

b. What fraction of the yachts are white?

c. How many yellow yachts are there?

10. Fill in the missing numbers.

$0.06 \div \boxed{} = 0.006$ $27.5 \div \boxed{} = 2.75$

$4.9 \div \boxed{} = 0.049$ $3.28 \div \boxed{} = 0.00328$

WORKING OUT AREA

MATHS

Test C
Booklet

11a

1 mark

11b

2 marks

11. Below are the heights of seven children at a party.

Cara	160cm
Eleanor	135cm
Jalam	150cm
Helen	145cm
Ross	130cm
Zoe	135cm
Lee	140cm

a. Which two children have the **modal** height?

_____

b. Which child has the **median** height value?
Show your working out.

_____

WORKING OUT AREA

c. On the line graph below draw in the height measurements for Jalam and Zoe.

11c

2 marks

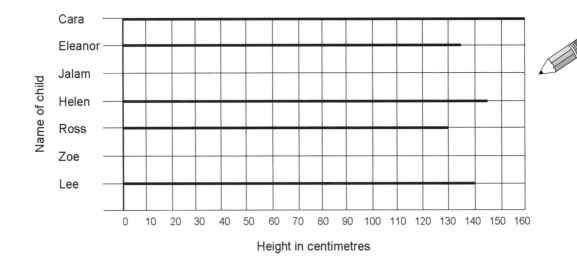

Height in centimetres

12. Change each amount into the unit that is shown.

12

4 marks

TOTAL

4.6cm = [   ] mm   3.55 litres = [   ] ml

7.45kg = [   ] g   4.5km = [   ] m

STOP HERE

6

11. Fill in the missing amount in each problem.

a. 33p + [ ] = 51p

e. [ ] + 46g = 92g

b. [ ] ÷ 4 = £5

f. 75p − [ ] = 50p

c. 40g − 16g = [ ]

g. £26 × 2 = [ ]

d. 3 × [ ] = 15

h. [ ] ÷ 2 = 39

11

4 marks

WORKING
OUT AREA

12. Swimming lessons last half an hour.

Write the missing times in the chart
to show the time of each child's lesson.

12

1 mark

Child's name	Starting time	Finishing time
Laura	10.45am	
David		1.45pm
Lisa		3.30pm
Sean	11.30am	

TOTAL

13a

1 mark

13b

1 mark

13c

1 mark

13. Work out the missing numbers in these function machines.

a.

In → 70 → × 4 → Out [ ]

b.

In [ ] → ÷ 5 → Out 10

c.

In 60 → − → Out 29

14. Look at this chart carefully. It shows the four main hair colours of the children in the three infant classes at North Road School.

	black	red	brown	blond
Class 1	7	8	12	3
Class 2	9	4	11	6
Class 3	8	2	9	5

14a

1 mark

a. How many children in Class 2 do not have red hair?

_____

14b

1 mark

b. Which class has four times as many children with black hair than with red hair?

_____

14c

1 mark

c. What is the total number of children in Class 1?

_____

10

15. The schedules below show the times of some popular television programmes. Look at them carefully and then answer the questions.

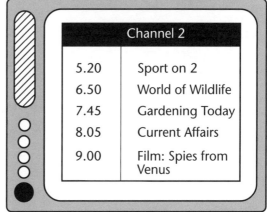

Channel 1	
6.00	World News
7.00	Chart Toppers
7.50	Motoring Now
8.10	Police in Action
8.40	Clown Time

Channel 2	
5.20	Sport on 2
6.50	World of Wildlife
7.45	Gardening Today
8.05	Current Affairs
9.00	Film: Spies from Venus

a. Which programme starts at 7.45 and ends at 8.05 on Channel 2?

15a

1 mark

_____

b. The comedy film on Channel 1 will last for $1\frac{3}{4}$ hours. At what time will the film finish?

15b

1 mark

_____

c. What programme will be showing at 8.05 on Channel 1?

15c

1 mark

_____

TOTAL

16a. Tick the sum that has the correct answer.

16a

1 mark

```
    3   6              9   4              5   2              4   7
  x     9            x     7            x     8            x     6
  ─────────          ─────────          ─────────          ─────────
  2   7   4          6   4   8          4   1   6          2   6   4
```

b. Fill in the missing numbers in this multiplication. Both numbers are the same.

c. Now fill in the missing numbers in this problem. Once again, both numbers are the same.

16b

1 mark

16c

1 mark

☐ × ☐ = 36

☐ × ☐ = 81

WORKING OUT AREA

17. Mark the position of these weights on the scale in the same way as the completed example has been done.

17

1 mark

150g

400g

600g

750g

```
0                          500g              1kg
├──┬──┬──┬──┬──┬──┬──┬──┬──▼──┬──┬──┬──┬──┬──┬──┬──┤
```

18. Study this graph and then answer the questions.

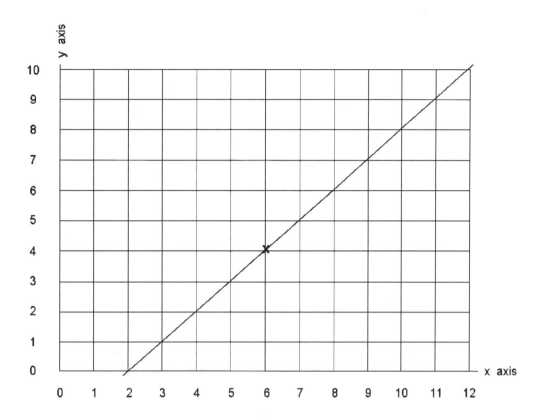

(6, 4) are the coordinates of the point marked **x** on the line.

a. Look at the coordinates below and tick those that are also points on the line.

(12, 10) ⬜   (6, 8) ⬜   (11, 9) ⬜

(4, 8) ⬜   (8, 6) ⬜   (5, 3) ⬜

18a

1 mark

b. Give any three coordinates on the grid that will form a triangle when they are joined up.

18b

1 mark

TOTAL

_____

19a. Write these numbers in order starting with the least.

2004   4020

4002   2040

4200   2400

19a

1 mark

least _____ most

b. 1.2 is marked on the number line. Mark **1.75** in the same way.

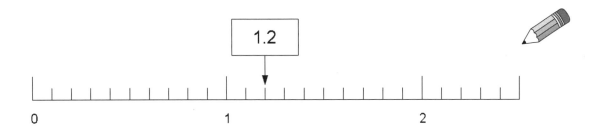

19b

1 mark

| 1.2 |

0   1   2

c. Complete these two-digit numbers so that each two-digit number is a multiple of 6. Then arrange the numbers in order, starting with the largest amount.

5   8   2

19c

1 mark

_____

WORKING
OUT AREA

14

20. Jim has a bag in which he places coloured counters. Read the statements below and then answer each question by choosing the most suitable word from the words listed in the box underneath.

> likely   impossible   certain   evens   unlikely

Jim puts ten red counters and ten blue counters in his bag.

a. What are the chances of him picking out a red counter first?

_____

20a

1 mark

Jim empties his bag and then places ten red counters and two green counters in his bag.

b. What are the chances of him picking out a green counter first?

_____

20b

1 mark

Jim empties his bag again and then fills it with yellow counters.

c. What are the chances of him picking out a red, blue or green counter?

_____

20c

1 mark

21. Fill in the missing digits in this calculation. There is more than one possible correct answer, but you only need to choose one to write down.

21

1 mark

TOTAL

| | 7 | 3 | + | | 6 | 5 | = 838 |

STOP HERE

15

Let's learn at home
MATHS

Test A
Booklet

Mental Arithmetic Test

CALCULATOR NOT ALLOWED

For this test you will need only a **pencil** or **pen**.
You are **NOT** allowed to use a **scrap piece of paper**, a **ruler**, a **calculator** or an **eraser**.

Marks
scored

Marks possible 20

Listen carefully to the instructions read out
to you at the beginning of the test.

Q Practice question

You will have five seconds for
each of these questions:

1.

2.

3.

4.

5.

You will have ten seconds for
each of these questions:

6.

7. mm

8. | 30 2 5

9. | 4.1 ↓ 4.7

Q

10. | 4 7 6 3

11. min

12. | 6 2 8 9

13.

14. cakes

15. p

You will have 15 seconds for
each of these questions:

16. | 50 14 7

17. | $2\frac{1}{2}$ 70p

18.

19. | 45 25 5 10

20. | 309 903

15. Award 1 mark each for a–c (credit answers with spelling mistakes). **3**

a. Gardening Today

b. 10.25

c. Motoring Now

(See tips for question 12.) You can help your child further with this type of question by giving him or her the page from a newspaper or magazine that contains the television schedules and asking similar styles of question to those in question 15. Answers could be given orally or in written form – whichever you feel is more appropriate.

16.

a. Award 1 mark if the third sum in the line is ticked. **1**

52 × 8 = 416

Award 1 mark each for b and c (only give credit if both the numbers in each calculation are the same).

b. 6 × 6 = 36 **2**

c. 9 × 9 = 81

Any oral or written activity that helps your child to learn the table facts to 10 × 10 will be of help with these types of calculation.

17. Award 1 mark for all three weights correctly positioned on the scale. **1**

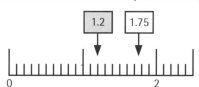

A scale is a type of 'number line'. It shows how numbers, in this case weights, are ordered. Asking questions such as 'What number lies half-way between 500 and 1000?' or 'What whole number is between 1234 and 1236?' are useful ways of stimulating your child to work mentally in this area of the curriculum.

18.

a. Award 1 mark if all the following coordinates are ticked (if five or all six boxes are ticked award no marks). **1**

(12, 10) (11, 9) (8, 6) (5, 3)

b. Award 1 mark if the three coordinates given will join up to form a triangle of any size on the grid (do not give credit for individual coordinates or numbers). For example: (0, 0), (4, 0), (4, 5) or (5, 2), (10, 6), (7, 7) and so on, would be creditworthy answers. **1**

Remind your child that the horizontal co-ordinate is always given before the vertical co-ordinate. A simple game of 'Battleships' is an enjoyable and beneficial way of helping your child to master the basics of co-ordinates. Identifying the position of features on a map or plan using the grid lines, perhaps while on a car journey or walking round a strange town, is another activity that will help your child to understand the practical use to which co-ordinates can be put.

19.

a. Award 1 mark if all the numbers are in the correct order. **1**

2004, 2040, 2400, 4002, 4020, 4200

b. Award 1 mark if the number is correctly positioned on the number line (use discretion). **1**

| 1.2 | 1.75 |

0   2

c. Award 1 mark if all three numbers are correct and arranged in the right order. **1**

54, 84, 24

84, 54, 24

Practise ordering groups of up to ten four-digit numbers starting with the least/most.

If your child had difficulty with this question then try and explain why the 1.75 goes where it does on the number line. Reference to place value will be necessary at this stage. Point out the differences in value between 175, 17.5, 1.75 and 0.175. If your child is showing signs of understanding, then ask him or her to mark on the line other amounts such as 0.25 or 1.35 or 2.45, and so on. (You might find reference to money useful in your explanation.) Encourage your child to mark the 'in-between' divisions on the line.

An ability to recall table facts is required to answer these questions. Give your child further questions of the same type to practise. Keep the amounts less than 100.

20. Award 1 mark each for a–c (credit answers with spelling mistakes). **3**

a. evens

b. unlikely

c. impossible

This question is about mathematical 'probability': the chance of something happening. You can help to improve your child's understanding of this topic by discussing whether a particular event is certain, very likely, likely, unlikely, very unlikely or impossible.

21. Award 1 mark for any of the options listed. **1**

173 + 665, 273 + 565, 373 + 465

473 + 365, 573 + 265, 673 + 165

This question can be done mentally but is really a pencil and paper calculation. To give your child experience of this type of problem, involving two missing digits, write out similar examples to those on the test sheet but arrange the numbers in traditional HTU columns to make the calculating process easier for your child to see what is going on. (You may find it quicker to do a complete sum first and then erase the two numbers you wish to leave out.)

Answers to Test B

Q	MARKS

1. Award 1 mark for each set of three correct answers in a and b. **2**
   a. 17, 4, 3
   b. 19, 51, 15

2. Award 1 mark each for a and b (do not credit answers with the p sign missing). **2**
   a. £1.60
   b. 40p

3.
   a. Award 1 mark if all three shapes are correctly marked. Only one 'x' is required in the first shape. **1**

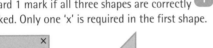

   b. Award 1 mark for each correct part of section b.   12, 6 **2**

   c. **1**
   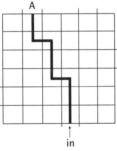
   in

4. Award 1 mark for a correctly completed block graph. **1**
   a.
   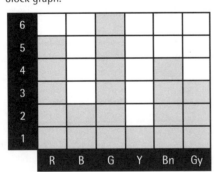

   Award 1 mark each for b and c. **2**
   b. 4
   c. 2

5. Award 1 mark if all the numbers are joined up correctly. **1**
   43, 42, 34, 32, 31, 24, 23, 21, 13, 12

Tips to help your child – Test B

A calculator can be used when answering any of the questions in this test. However, it will not necessarily be needed to make all of the questions easier. Part of the skill of using a calculator is to know when to use it.

Practise using the four rules of number working within these ranges: add/subtract single-digit numbers to/from two-digit numbers without crossing the tens (without 'borrowing'); multiply/divide numbers in the 2, 3, 4, 5 and 10 times tables as far as ×10.

There are many occasions when you can help your child to improve his or her confidence in dealing with money. Practical activities at home using the lower denomination coins is an obvious example. Adding up the cost of several small value purchases in a newsagents leading to working out how much change from a pound is another. Asking your child to check the figures on a till receipt using a calculator is also a valuable exercise.

In order to answer questions about angles your child will need to know some of the vocabulary associated with this area of mathematics. You can help your child by making sure that he or she understands the meanings of terms such as *north, south, east, west, north-east, north-west, south-east, south-west, clockwise, anti-clockwise, acute angle, straight angle* and *obtuse angle*.

This question requires your child to carry out the two operations of counting and subtracting. On squared paper draw some empty grids that all contain squares in multiples of ten (for example, 5 × 8, 5 × 10, 6 × 10 and so on) up to a maximum of 100 squares. Ask your child to shade in a given number of squares and to then subtract that amount from the total number of squares in the grid.
Practise additional directional activities with your child using squared paper. As well as words such as 'forwards', 'backwards' and 'sideways', introduce the expressions 'left' and 'right'.

If your child had difficulty with this question, explain to him or her how to transfer the information from the table to the block graph. Having done this, change the amounts in the 'Number of cars' column on the table and ask your child to now transfer this altered information onto a newly drawn block graph.
Both of the questions in sections b and c are subtraction problems. Try to explain to your child that terms such as 'how many more than', 'how many less than', 'find the difference between' and so on, all require subtraction calculation.

Practise ordering groups of up to ten two-digit numbers starting with the lowest/highest.

6. Award 1 mark for all three questions
answered correctly.
31
Sunday
3rd, 10th, 17th, 24th, 31st (also credit just the
numbers on their own).

1

A range of further problems similar to those found in
this question can be made up for use with your child.
Also, make sure that he or she commits to memory the
number of days in a year/leap year, the number of weeks
in a year, the number of days in a week and the number
of days in each month.

7. Award 1 mark each for a–c.
a. 3, 9, 15, 21, 27 (the cross-over section)
b. 6, 12, 18, 24, 30 (the bottom section)
c. 6, 12, 18, 24, 30 (the bottom section)

3

Explain that any numbers that are within both circles
must be both odd numbers and multiples of 3. See if
your child can now draw a Venn diagram for even
numbers and multiples of 3 with 30 as the largest
number on the diagram.

8. Award 1 mark each for a–d (the £ sign must
be shown to make the answer creditworthy).
a. £19.00
b. £16.50
c. £21.50
d. £17.00

4

To reinforce the kind of activity presented by this
question, you could ask your child to use the entrance
fee information from a tourist attraction leaflet to work
out the cost of visiting the venue for a specified number
of adults and children.

9.
a. Award 1 mark for a correctly completed table.

1

flat faces only	curved faces only	flat and curved faces
cuboid cube pyramid	sphere	cylinder cone

b. Award 1 mark for naming any ball-shaped
object, for example, football, globe (credit apple/
orange or other items that are 'nearly' sphere
shaped).

1

Your child should be familiar with the names and
properties of all six solid figures referred to in the
question. He or she should be able to identify each of
these solid figures from a written or oral description of
their key features. In addition, your child should also be
able to do the same with a prism and cone. When you
are out take the opportunity to ask your child if he or
she can point out any features that display these
particular solid figure shapes.

10. Award 1 mark each for a and b.
a. 7
b. 14

2

Emphasize to your child that to find a half of an amount
you share by 2, to find a quarter you share by 4, to find a
third you share by 3, and so on. Begin to explain how a
remainder can be expressed as a fraction of the divisor,
for example $34 \div 5 = 6 \text{ r } 4$ or $\frac{4}{5}$.

11. Award 1 mark each for a–c.
a. 450 rounders
b. 150 rounders
c. 150 rounders

3

Check that your child has not overlooked the key that
accompanies the pictogram. Doing so will result in all
the answers being incorrect. Give your child practice at
adding HTU multiples of 10 mentally, using a pencil and
paper and a calculator. Allow him/her to find halves and
quarters of the answers using the same three methods.

12. Award 1 mark each for both a and b if each
calculation is connected to the correct answer.
a. $80 \div 10 = 8$, $15 + 45 = 60$,
$130 - 31 = 99$
b. $57 - 27 = 30$, $23 + 12 = 35$,
$24 \div 3 = 8$, $2 \times 11 = 22$

2

Revision work for problems like the ones in this question
can be tackled in the following way. First, ask your child
to guess roughly what he or she thinks the answer
should be. Write it down. Then get him or her to work
out the question mentally. Write that answer down.
When this has been done, ask your child to check his/her
mental answer using a pencil and paper method. Finally,
let your child check that answer using a calculator.

13. Award 1 mark each for a–c.
a. three hundred and fifty
b. 700
c. 437

3

Allow your child the opportunity to round other three-
digit numbers to the nearest 10 or 100. Move on to four-
digit numbers as soon as your child is competent to do
so. Remind your child that if a number is exactly half-
way between a whole 10 or 100 then the number is
rounded up, for example, 45 would be rounded to 50
and 450 would be rounded to 500. Also give your child
further practice at arranging three different digits to
make six different HTU numbers. If your child finds this
difficult mentally, write the digits onto small pieces of
paper at first so he/she can move the numbers around.

| Q | Answers | MARKS | Tips |

14. Award 1 mark each for a and b.   **2**
a. check grid for answer (2 parts)
b. square

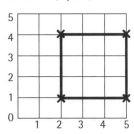

Remind your child that the horizontal co-ordinate is always given before the vertical co-ordinate. Then ask him or her to carry out these instructions. Draw and number a grid the same as the one on the page. Draw a map of a 'Treasure island' on the grid and mark on the map important features, including the position of the treasure. Underneath the grid write the names of the features marked on the map. Next to the name of each feature write the grid reference of where that feature can be found.

15. Award 1 mark each for a and b.   **2**
a. 500
b. 5750

Although your child may be able to work out the correct answers to this question mentally or by using pencil and paper methods, a more efficient way to obtain the result is to use a calculator.

16. Award 1 mark each for a and b (do not credit   **2**
answers that have the units of measure missing).
a. 2.3m (credit 2.30m, 2m 30cm, 230cm)
b. 2880mm (credit 288cm, 2.88m, 2m 88cm)

As with question 15, it is possible that your child will manage to work out the answers to this question without the aid of a calculator. However, a calculator would be the most time-effective way to tackle the problems involved. Both sections of this question require your child to hold an interim number.

17. Award 1 mark for any shape that has a total   **1**
outside edge measurement of 32cm. For example:

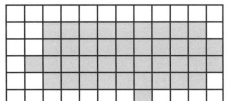

Many children find this task difficult. If your child falls into this category let him or her practise on cm² paper. Start by asking for perimeters of a short distance (5–10cm) and gradually work up to a maximum distance of about 50 cm. See if your child can tell you why some numbers seem harder to do than others.

18. Award 1 mark for each correctly completed   **2**
column of the table.

Number of daisies	Tally	Frequency
0–8	I	1
9–16	IIII	4
17–24	IIII	4
25–32	⊞I	6

Frequency charts present problems for many children mainly because they do not understand what they have to do. Explain that the word 'tally' means 'a mark to indicate a counted item' (for example, /// = 3) and 'frequency' means 'the total number of times something occurs' or 'the total number in a set or range'.

19. Award 1 mark each for a–c (credit answers   **3**
with spelling mistakes but do not credit answers
that have the £ sign missing).
a. football, trainers, bats (in any order)
b. £3.92
c. £11.00

The use of a calculator is strongly recommended in this question. The practical skills with which to answer this type of question can be acquired by your child if you let him or her use a calculator when out on a shopping trip.

20. Award 1 mark each for a and b.   **2**
a. 7 coaches
b. £480 (do not credit answers with the £ sign missing.)

The practical suggestions given for Q19 also apply here.

21. Award 1 mark each for a and b.   **2**
a. 74
b. 6

Make up sets of missing number questions for your child. Use any numbers under 100 and multiples of five or ten for amounts larger than this. Allow your child to answer the questions using either a calculator or pencil and paper methods. Emphasize that if you know two numbers in a calculation you can always find the third by carrying out one of the remaining four rules of number with the two numbers that you know.

22. Award 1 mark each for a and b.   **2**
a. 17
b. 7

The first sequence is: 3 + 2 = 5, 5 + 3 = 8, 8 + 4 = 12 and so on. The second sequence is: 25 – 6 = 19, 19 – 5 = 14, 14 – 4 = 10 and so on.

Answers to Test C

Q		MARKS
1.	Award 1 mark for each correct answer.	4
a.	177	
b.	231	
c.	3990	
d.	3015	

2.	Award 1 mark if both numbers are correct.	1
	13, 17	

3.
a. Award 1 mark for each correct answer (credit **2** the answer if the units of measure are missing).
2000cm (20m) 56 600m (56.6km)
b. Award 1 mark for each correct answer (credit **2** the answer if the units of measure are missing).
6000g (6kg) £50 000
c. Award 1 mark for each correct answer **2** providing the calculation has been worked out along the lines shown. (There are several other 'new' methods being introduced these days, so don't be surprised if your child does these calculations in a way you do not recognize.)

```
        1  3  5              ┌─────────
    ×      2  9       4  5 │ 6  7  5
    ─────────────          ┌─────────
    2  7  0  0             4  5
                           ─────────
    1  2  1  5             2  2  5
    ─────────────          2  2  5
    3  9  1  5             ─────────
                           0  0  0
```

4. Award 1 mark each for a and b. **2**
a. 228
b. 252

5. Award 1 mark each for a–d. **4**
a. 142.5cm²
b. 60cm²
c. 49cm
d. 40cm

Q		MARKS

6. Award 1 mark each for a–c (do not credit **3** answers with the units of measure missing).
a. 26°C
b. 11°C
c. 25°C

7. Award 1 mark each for a and b. **2**
a. 30° (accept 29° or 31°)
b. acute

8. Award 2 marks for any set of four numbers **2** that add up to 28.

9. Award 1 mark each for a–c. **3**
a. 25%
b. one third ($\frac{1}{3}$)
c. 36

10. Award 1 mark for each correct answer. **4**
10, 10
100, 1000

11.
a. Award 1 mark for the names of both children. **1**
Eleanor, Zoe
b. Award 1 mark for 'Lee' and 1 mark for **2** evidence of working out that would indicate that the heights of the children have been arranged in order and the child with the middle height chosen (do not credit a mark for the name of the child if there is no evidence of how this was arrived at).
c. Award 1 mark for each correctly drawn line **2** on the graph.

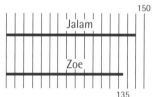

12. Award 1 mark for each correct answer. **4**
46mm, 3550ml
7450g, 4500m

Answers to Mental

Arithmetic Test

Q		
p.24	Award 1 mark for each correct answer	
1.	7	
2.	4p	
3.	5	
4.	10	
5.	18	
6.	26	
7.	20	
8.	20	

Q	
9.	4.4
10.	20
11.	10
12.	13
13.	15
14.	3
15.	36
16.	29
17.	175p or £1.75
18.	120
19.	65
20.	100

INSTRUCTIONS FOR THE MENTAL ARITHMETIC TEST

You will need Test Paper A for your child (the grid for the answers is on page 16) and a clock or a watch that measures accurately in seconds.

Read out the following instructions to your child in a relaxed and friendly manner at the start of the test. Answer any questions that your child might ask.

This test has 20 questions and will only last for about 5 minutes. Each question will be read out to you twice. You must work out the answers to the questions in your head but you can jot things down outside the answer box if this is helpful to you. Make sure you write your answer in the box alongside the correct question number. For some questions, useful information to help your memory is given to you next to the answer box. As you work through the test the questions get harder but you will be allowed more time to work out the answers. If you want to change an answer, put a cross through your first answer and write your second answer next to the answer box. If you find a question too difficult, put a cross in the answer box and wait for the next question to be read out. You must not ask any questions once the test has started.

Reading out the questions

The questions should be read out to your child in a clear and precise manner and the working out times allowed for each group of questions should be strictly adhered to. It is a good idea to read through the questions beforehand so that when you are asking your child the questions for real your delivery is smooth and confident. Read each question twice allowing only a short pause between each reading. At the start of each timed group of questions tell your child how long they have to work out the answers to that group of questions. The time allowed for each question should begin as soon as you have finished reading the question for the second time. Read out the practice question first and use this as a warm-up for both you and your child. (Don't forget to start your timing as soon as you have read the question for the second time!) Finally, check that your child has written the practice question answer in the correct box on the answer page, answer any further queries your child might have and then begin the test.

MENTAL ARITHMETIC TEST

Read out all questions twice.

PQ. Write twenty-four in figures.

Say: You will have 5 seconds to answer each
of these questions.

1. Add together four and three.
2. Take away 6p from 10p.
3. How many tens in fifty?
4. Make five twice the size.
5. What number is eight more than ten?

Say: You will have 10 seconds to answer each of these questions.

6. Half of a number is thirteen. What is the number?
7. Two centimetres is the same length as how many millimetres?
8. Divide 30 by 2 and then add five.
9. On your answer sheet is a scale. Write down the number shown by the arrow.
10. What is the total of four, seven, six and three?

11. How many minutes from 9.55am to 10.05am?
12. Subtract six from the sum of two, eight and nine.
13. Find the difference between 6 × 5 and 3 × 5.
14. How many cakes are left over when 23 cakes are shared among four people?
15. What will be the cost of nine chews at 4p each?

Say: You will have 15 seconds to answer each of these questions.

16. How many less than fifty is 14 plus 7?
17. Find the cost of 2 $\frac{1}{2}$ litres of lemonade if one litre costs 70p.
18. Multiply eighty by six and write down a quarter of your answer.
19. To the sum of 45 and 25 subtract the difference between five and ten.
20. How many times greater is the three in 309 than the three in 903?

Say: The test is over. Put down your pen/ pencil.

MATHS
Practice for
Key Stage 2
National tests
ges 10-11

TEST
YOUR CHILD'S
MATHS

Parent's Booklet

Using this book. About National Tests
How to set up the test. Marking the
answers. Finding the level

Test A and Mental Arithmetic
Test Booklet pull-out

Test B and Test C Booklet pull-out

Let's learn at home
MATHS

INTRODUCTION

What are the Key Stage 2 National Tests?

Every year in May, children in Year 6 (the final year of primary school or midway through middle school) take written National Tests. There are two English, three maths and two science tests. They are designed to show the levels of work your child is able to achieve in these three core subjects. The tests are carried out over one week. The papers are marked by external examiners. When returned to school, the results of the tests (commonly known as SATs) give parents and teachers an indication of each child's knowledge in relation to the standards set out in the National Curriculum (NC). They also provide a rough guide to how your child's school has performed in relation to other schools both locally and nationally.

What the test results mean

Along with assessments made by the class teacher, your child's National Test results will be sent to his or her secondary school and be used by the staff there to help them decide the most appropriate teaching groups for your child to be placed in.

About the maths tests

During the test week, your child will take three separate maths tests at school. The first two (Tests A and B) will each last 45 minutes and be taken on different days. The third is a mental arithmetic test with about 20 quick-fire questions with varying times allowed for answering. These tests cover NC Levels 3–5 and the questions increase in difficulty through the paper. Under exceptional circumstances, and at the discretion of the teacher, a very able child can be entered for an additional Level 6 extension test lasting 30 minutes (Test C).

The mathematics National Curriculum is divided up into: (Ma1) Using and Applying Mathematics; (Ma2) Number; (Ma3) Shape, Space and Measures; (Ma4) Handling Data. Each section has a Programme of Study setting out what should be taught and Attainment Targets for expected standards or levels of performance. This is mirrored in the test structure.

The National Tests exclude the testing of 'Using and Applying Mathematics' and concentrate on testing your child's knowledge and understanding of number, shape and data handling. 'Using and Applying Mathematics' will be assessed by your child's class teacher, but is still very important. The sections do not have equal proportions of the test marks. In Tests A and B, 'Number' has the most questions and accounts for nearly half of the total number of marks available on the test papers. 'Shape, Space and Measures' and 'Handling Data' share about an equal proportion of the remaining questions and marks. The mental arithmetic marks account for about 20 per cent (one fifth) of the total marks available in the tests.

How this book can help you to help your child

The practice papers in this book can help you prepare your child in the most realistic way possible for the end of Key Stage 2 National Tests in maths. They will help to:

- familiarize your child with the format and layout of test papers
- familiarize your child with the type of questions in the tests
- indicate areas of strength or weakness
- approximate for you the level your child is working at in maths.

The 'Tips to Help Your Child' notes which accompany the answers to Tests A and B provide suggestions for ways in which you can help to improve your child's progress and performance, not only with the questions on the test papers, but also in associated mathematical areas.